To Dad

Merry Christmas

Love

Jo & Ken

XX

Special thanks to American Express®, and Buckingham Group Contracting Limited without whom this book would not have been possible

A big thank you... to all of the companies that helped build our stadium:

A C Flooring
Adenstar Developments Ltd
AFL Architects
AJM E&P Solutions
Amos White Lining
AMPM
Andy Blunden
Anti-Graffiti Systems
APiC
Amey
Arup
ASB Law
Ascent Lifts
Associated Asphalt
Astore Harrison
Austin Cradles
Azure
Bang & Olufsen
Beach Soil Stabilisation
Berry Piling
Bespoke Precast
Bespoke Property Ltd
BGCL
Bioworks
Blue Cube
Bonhams
Brighton & Hove City Council
Brilliant Orange Sports Management
Broadway Malyan
Broadway Systems
Buckingham Group Contracting Ltd
CA Group
CA Roofing
Carrino
CEP
CIC
Clean Event
CMS Catering
Colourworks
Concept Sealants
Corbeau
Daktronics
Davis Arnold Cooper
DMH Stallard
Drywall Construction
Dudman Concrete Limited
Edward Doe
EK Span
Elliott Brickwork
Empire Stadiums
Errea
European Door Sets
European Office Products
Everest & Miles
Faithfull & Gould
Fortress
Franklin & Andrews
G&A Fire Protection / Drywall
Garran
Giffords
GPB Mastic
Graffiti Designs
Graham Barrie Designs
Grout Injection Specialist
Halcrow Yolles
HBPW
Helmsley Orrell Partnership
Hennigan
HIS
Hyland Edgar Driver
Icon / Graffiti
Intrad
IPT Design
Iron Designs
IT First
Jaysam
JCS Cleaning
JLA
Kaba
Kattenhorn
KCCJ
Kestrel
Kestral Contractors
KSS Architects
KSS Interiors
Leigh's Paints
Lockers & Benches
LondonWall
M25 Contracting Ltd
Macrete Ireland
Magicman
Manual Handling
Mass Installations
May Gurney
ME Engineers
Michael Cook Associates
MK Building Control
MQM
N-Class
Natural PR
N G Bailey
NSure
Oliver Overhead Door Company
Overline
Parker Building Supplies
PCS Technology
Peer Spanner Associates
P J Saines / RAB Carpentry
Planet Partitions
Prestige
PWC
Reading Agricultural Consultants
RH Consulting
Road Grip
Robinson Low Francis
Rowecast
Seeda
Sequoia
Shotcrete
Siemens Plc
S J Berwin
SKM Engineers
SmithsGore
South Coast Glazing
Specialist Lining Systems
SRJ Fencing
SSW Fencing
Steve Rooke
Sussex Signs
System Geotechnique
Talent
TCL
Tenos
The Healthy Company
Total Laminates
Tripleplay
TSL
TUSC
UK Sports Products
Universal Safety Systems
Vanguardia
Volvina
Watson Steelwork
Webb Yates Engineering
White Young Green
Whitings
Wingate Electrical
Yannadis

First published in 2011 by Step Beach Press Limited,
28 Osborne Villas, Hove BN3 2RE, UK

ISBN: 978-1-908779-00-7

Design by Itonic Design, Brighton
Photography by Paul Hazlewood, Laura Collins and Graeme Rolf
Printed and bound in Malta
Manufacturing Managed by Jellyfish Solutions Ltd.

Acknowledgements

Buckingham Group Contracting Limited for supporting the production of this book, having spent three years constructing our new home.

American Express, our stadium sponsors, who also provided generous support to make this book happen.

Tony Bloom, Chairman, for stepping in to ensure this iconic landmark became a reality.

Martin Perry, Chief Executive, for his persistence in first winning planning permission, then overseeing the entire build process, and providing commentary throughout this publication.

Derek Chapman, Director, for overseeing the construction process, as well as providing some of the breathtaking aerial images from his helicopter.

Dick Knight, Life President, for saving the club from extinction and working shoulder to shoulder with Martin to obtain that initial planning permission.

Last but by no means least, all of you who were involved in the fight to save our club at any point between 1995 and 2008. Without you, this club would not be where it is today.

All profits from this book are being donated to Albion in the Community. Albion in the Community helps people, young and old, across Sussex and further afield, with innovative projects and initiatives that inspire, educate and motivate.

Tony Bloom

Like all the best modern day squads, this book consists of a selection of forewords. And Gus Poyet certainly is right, every good squad needs numerous good ones!

As you leaf through these amazing images, you may, like me, be struck by the enormity of the task Martin and Derek faced in creating an image for our dream. They assembled a team in KSS (our architects) and Buckingham (our constructors) who have delivered a stadium that is truly world class.

Despite all the misfortune we had to endure in finding ourselves a home, we have been blessed by leaders with talent and fight. In 1997 Dick stepped in to take over and save the club when there was no one else to do so. Without his courage and vision we would not be where we are today.

Martin gets the prize for endurance. His toil was a decade long campaign for the effective survival of the football club, as without a home, no club can survive. He became quite well known to various Council members over the course of thirty-odd planning meetings. He could have a second career as a lobbyist and a third in Public Relations.

Derek from the outset has been in complete control of the construction phase. His commercialism and far-sightedness continue to stand us in good stead; the conception of this book, and the idea of putting something back into the community by channelling it through Albion in the Community, is one of his many contributions.

So the images here only show the tail-end of the task, but it was some task. Few boards could boast the construction capabilities of Martin and Derek combined. They certainly have formed a formidable partnership. I cannot think of many projects on the scale of the Amex which have come in on time and, but for a few extras like the padded seats, on budget. We are the first stadium to have received a 'BREEAM' rating which speaks of the environmentally friendly approach we have taken. We have created thousands of jobs in the local area, and we source locally wherever possible and recycle money back in to the local community.

The name of our stadium, the American Express Community Stadium, is extremely important. The stadium was built for football, and created for the community. Albion in the Community (AITC) is one of the strongest football community schemes in the UK. We continue to be awed by the effect football can have in delivering messages, educating communities and improving self-esteem. Our stadium is a facility for AITC to give back to the community that supports us. No club in the world has a stronger stadium sponsor than the Albion with American Express. They are one of the world's most high profile brands and are also hugely involved in the local community, and we are privileged to be partners with them.

Whilst we do all we can to offer superb entertainment to our fans and a living breathing stadium to the county and the community, the real business is done on the pitch. We look forward to developing an academy and first-class training facilities over the next few years to give our first-team players and youngsters the facilities to improve and thrive. In 35 years of supporting Brighton & Hove Albion, I have not previously seen the quality and class that the team has shown over the last 18 months. Gus Poyet is an inspirational manager and leader, and is laying the foundations for our football team to play a certain style of football for many years to come.

My grandfather Harry was Vice-Chairman of the club in the 1970s and my uncle Ray has more than 20 years of Albion boardroom experience. For over half a century, three generations of Bloom living rooms have borne witness to discussion over great incidents of our footballing history. My father also encouraged me throughout my childhood to improve my geography by visiting many away grounds!

The Amex will provide many exciting moments, triumphs and heartaches for many, many decades to come. Every time I come to the stadium, I take huge satisfaction from what so many of us have achieved to get here. I marvel at the splendid surrounding area and the design which blends in so beautifully with the rolling Downs.

Please enjoy the book and I look forward to creating many special memories with you in the future.

Martin Perry

"We need men who can dream of things that never were"
John F Kennedy

On Saturday 26th April 1997 Brighton & Hove Albion played Doncaster Rovers. It was the last game played at the Goldstone Ground and after the game we sheltered in the boardroom whilst outside the fans were dismantling the old ground for souvenirs.

Fourteen years later on 6th August 2011 Brighton & Hove Albion played Doncaster Rovers again, the first League game to be played at the American Express Community Stadium.

I had the privilege to be at both of those games even though 14 years passed between them, looking back, it seems as though the time went by almost without noticing. And yet so much happened in that period.

The club played at four Football League grounds – the Goldstone, the Priestfield, Withdean and the Amex. We went from the very bottom of the Football League into the Championship and won three titles and four promotions, including a Play-off final on the way. But quite apart from the rollercoaster ride on the field there was enough activity off the field to fill several books, let alone this one!!

I still remember the day when I was invited up to Village Way by the then Director of Finance of the University of Brighton and shown the site for the first time – I saw immediately the potential and that belief never wavered. I remember writing the shared vision paper which set out how each of the major stakeholders would benefit from the development of a new stadium on this site and the more we looked into it the stronger the case became.

Our new home has now become a reality because so many people shared in that vision. No single person delivered this stadium. It was because a group of amazing people came together – Dick, Tony, Derek, the wonderful team of designers, engineers and builders, including the lawyers! But above all the fans who "got it". They all understood, shared in that vision and pulled together and the result is something very very special.

I am so proud and privileged to have been part of an amazing journey and thank everyone who has supported us. Together we have created a legacy not just for Brighton & Hove Albion but for the City of Brighton & Hove.

It never was just about football – it was much more important than that!

Dick Knight

From the moment it was announced I was taking over the Albion back in its darkest times in 1997, a few days before the last ever game at the Goldstone, I had two idealistically simple objectives on my mind:

Save the club. Deliver a wonderful, new permanent home for the Albion.

After all I'd been through in the long battle to unseat my notorious predecessor, Bill Archer, surely those two hugely worthwhile goals would be a relative piece of cake...

The first part was always going to happen. What inspired me as a boy was watching an all-time Albion great, the mesmerising Johnny McNichol. What inspired me as a man was to save the club – for future generations of children. I had my determination, my vision, my money – above all I had the fans with me in our quest.

From the beginning my vision for the stadium was based on it being, not just a new home for the Albion, but a state-of-the-art arena for the community providing a range of public services. That's why, back in 2001, the building was registered as "The Community Stadium".

Throughout the years of toil, that vision never faltered. And when we finally gained stadium approval – thanks largely to the supreme efforts of those fans – I was delighted that American Express shared our community vision for our magnificent new stadium. It has proved a tremendous partnership.

There are so many people to thank on that memorable road to the Amex. Martin, Derek and Tony, of course. The Falmer For All team and countless thousands of other Albion supporters... You all played a part. You all made it happen. That's why this stadium is so very different than any other – it had an unbelievable history before a ball was kicked. And, like me, you can tell your grandchildren that it was worth it.

Thank you.

Derek Chapman

A great man once said "I have a dream". Well so did I, but my dream became reality and I helped make it happen.

I first had this dream on 26th April 1997 at 16.52, when the final whistle sounded to bring an end to the Albion v Doncaster game and signalled the end of our home of 95 years. The dream was realised on 6th August 2011 when, through tearful eyes, I watched the Albion walk out on to the pitch at the American Express Community Stadium (sorry but the Spurs game didn't count!). Suddenly the 14 years in between seemed to disappear in a flash.

The stadium is literally "close to home" for me; I attended school half a mile away. I now live in Falmer and when I started my own business the first job I worked on was in the University of Sussex. So when the decision was made to build the stadium in Falmer I may have been the only local who was happy! (There may have been others, but to my knowledge I was the only one who publicly stated the fact.) In fact I am a GIMBY (great in my back yard) and not a NIMBY!

The stadium is a testament to what two very stubborn people (Martin and Dick), our fans who never stopped believing and a special Albion hero (Tony) can achieve. As they say, "Fans united will never be defeated," and we weren't!

Sometimes it was difficult to believe it would happen. I remember board meetings in the early 2000s when we would spend eight hours discussing how we were going to pay the next month's wages, and then end the meetings discussing the design of our £60 million (at the time) stadium development, or that we couldn't afford to sign a new player as we needed the cash to pay the architect or engineer to produce information for the planning inquiry!

My bit of fun came in the last two and a half years, selecting the builder and overseeing the construction. It only seems like yesterday when we had the ground breaking ceremony (remember Dick missed his penalty?). That was also the day my dad died. Then Village Way being completed. Our fans chasing the first section of the East Stand roof arch down the A23 and posting pictures on the net. The first seat being fixed and 12 of us on our hands and knees inspecting the first blades of grass that grew on the pitch. It all seems to have passed in the blink of an eye.

The builders were great; I have made friends who will last my lifetime. This was no Wembley; we finished on time and on budget. I still drive around the A27 worrying that all I will see is the University buildings and a grass field and that I had fallen asleep in one of our all day board meetings and in fact it has all been a dream!!

Building the stadium is MY legacy in MY home city. In years to come my grandchildren (if I have any) will know that their granddad helped build this stadium. In the past cities built great cathedrals to worship in... now we build stadiums.

So to Martin, Dick, Tony and all our fans...

Thank you and enjoy.

Paul Hazlewood

Having been involved in first the fight to save the club during the end of the Goldstone era, then the campaign to "Bring Home the Albion", I cannot fully articulate what finally moving into the Amex really means to me. Words wouldn't do it justice. What I can say is that Tony Bloom, Martin Perry, Derek Chapman and Dick Knight, together with all of you who joined in any of the campaigns, are all owed a huge debt of gratitude by the many thousands who can now enjoy watching their team in this state-of-the-art stadium for the community.

It has taken time, patience, resolve and endeavour, but together we got there in the end. What drives that home to me is a very personal thing, because it represents a missing generation. My son was just six months old when I took him to the Goldstone Ground. It was a moment of madness really, amidst all the turmoil going on at the time, but I just felt it was something I had to do. I never missed a game at the Priestfield, but I'd not have forced that onto him! Then at the age of five I bought him his first season ticket at Withdean, and there he stayed only ever knowing the South Stand for the next 10 years. So, now taking his place, aged 15, amongst 20,000 in this breathtaking arena, I know he's earned his right of passage.

Being given free rein by Martin and Richard Hebberd (Operations Manager), to document photographically the build process is something I consider to be a huge honour, and I hope that together with Laura and Graeme, we have truly captured the essence of the construction.

Being afforded such intimate access is something that I'm sure any Albion fan, whether interested in photography or not, would have given their right arm for. It is of course a privilege and having been in and around the place as it grew from a muddy field into what you see before you today, is something that I will remember for the rest of my life. With that also came a feeling of real responsibility. This book, I hope, will become a tiny piece of Albion history, and perhaps a hundred years from now, my great-great-grandchildren – or yours – might find a copy in the loft, dust it down and thumb through the pages in much the same way as we all do on occasion with old family photo albums.

Personally, this is the first time in my career as a photographer that I have worked on a construction project. Most photographers consider themselves specialists in weddings, commercial, events, portraiture, architecture. I love to photograph people, so throughout the build, I've always kept (not literally of course!) one eye on the construction and the other on the lookout for interesting images of people at work.

There have been many great moments... the first steel being set, the arches going up, cladding, pitch seeding, handing over of the keys, the first major event in the Platinum Lounge (when the place truly came alive for the first time), naming rights day... the list is vast.

Of the many thousands of images captured throughout the time, it would be easy to say that the covershot – the moment when like many of you, my emotions were wrecked and I was finally reduced to tears – would be the one that stood out the most. For me however, the outstanding memory will always be the day I struggled across to the site through a snowy blizzard, in truly Arctic conditions when the rest of the country deemed it more appropriate to take a "duvet day", to see workers engulfed in layers of clothing amidst snowdrifts, elevated in cherry pickers painting sections of the East Stand arch, whilst others worked heavy machinery still going about their business. I was, once again, lost for words. I'd only made the effort to get an external shot of our new home in a picture postcard snow scene, but now I could see that nothing was going to prevent the stadium from being delivered on time for the start of the new season. I'd have cried at that moment too if I had any feeling left in my face, fingers or feet!

I'll close by reiterating how I began. To "the men of steel", Tony, Martin, Derek and Dick, thank you for delivering this wonderful sporting arena and bringing pride, a home, and a genuine future back to our football club, and to all of you who fought the fight, for never giving up the battle, never losing sight of the dream, and doing all of that with dignity, style, ingenuity and at times a real sense of humour in the face of adversity.

It is true what they say, "everything comes to he (or she) who waits".

Laura Collins

When I first joined the Albion in 2007 I was completely unaware of the struggle the club had been through to survive. I had heard of the plans to build a new stadium in Falmer but had little opinion on the matter.

During my role as PA to Martin Perry the full story was explained to me and I realised just how close to the brink the club had come. If not for the determination of key individuals Martin Perry, Dick Knight, Derek Chapman and Tony Bloom there may not have been a story to tell at all.

Working closely with Martin I quickly became involved in all aspects of the stadium project, visiting the site when it was just a muddy brown field. It was on one of these visits that I remember Martin standing in the middle of an overgrown pathway in the University of Brighton telling me that it was the exact spot where one of the goals would be placed. It was difficult to visualise at the time and it all seemed such a long way off. Less than three years later there I was again, this time stood behind the goalmouth to photograph the official handover of the stadium by contractors Buckingham Group. I almost couldn't believe the change that had taken place.

Before any construction works commenced on site a full archaeological survey was carried out in September 2008. It was then I began to photograph the site, my intention to provide a record for the club and offer an inside view posting images on the club website. For the next two and a half years I would continue to regularly document all developments come rain, shine... or snow!

I was lucky enough to witness key moments during the stadium construction but my most memorable was the official ground breaking of the site aptly named the "Kick-off ceremony". On an icy cold morning in December 2008 three buses made their way over to Falmer carrying individuals involved in the long campaign to find the club a new home. The ceremony entailed the Chairman at the time, Dick Knight, and Chief Executive Martin Perry taking a penalty shoot-out at a goal created from two diggers with arms extended to create a crossbar. This made for a slightly unconventional way to carry out the ceremony but was also perfectly fitting. Among the group were those who had petitioned and worked tirelessly for years on this cause and by the smiles on everyone's faces I could see how much the day meant.

I feel extremely privileged to have been involved in this key episode in Albion history and feel proud that I have been able to contribute to this project as an Albion employee and photographer. I hope this book stands as proof of what can be achieved through perseverance, hard work and huge commitment to a dream.

Finally, to all Albion fans out there, welcome home.

Graeme Rolf

With my office based in Stanmer Park, each day, at least once, I would need to drive up the slip road by the University in order to head back to Brighton. Even before permission was finally given to build our stadium (I always believed it would happen), I used to look longingly at the farmer's field opposite each time I sat patiently in the queue approaching the roundabout. Any passengers with me would know what I was going to say; after all, I said the same thing time and time again after looking over to my right. I used to say it even if I was on my own. "Once work starts over there, I will take photos every week, right the way until the stadium is finished."

In October 2008, I spotted a lone, not overly large digger, pecking away in the field. "This must be it!" I thought. Out came my trusty little Sony Cybershot digital camera. I always had it on me as I have to take photos of various bits of Brighton's greenery as part of my job. There can't be many Albion fans in my position, basically being paid each day to monitor progress of the build? I felt an overwhelming compunction to share my good fortune. What better way than to put the photos on the internet? Being a member of North Stand Chat, I put them on there."Jack Straw's Falmer Watch" was born.

It transpired that the diggers were just carrying out archaeological surveys, so as to make sure that there was no invaluable history being consigned to a grave with a football stadium as a head-stone. I wasn't keen on Baldrick and his band of beardy hairys holding up progress. It had taken 12 years to get this far.

Early in 2009, the widening of Village Way started. Never before have I been so excited about tarmac, and probably never again. Viewings of my photos started to increase, and I was averaging about five hundred hits per week. As the road works neared completion, what is now the coach park started to appear, along with dozens of Portakabins. Now call me sad, but now I'd bore people by wittering on about Portakabins.

Huge lorries full of chalk now trundled relentlessly across from the farmer's field to the field opposite. I sometimes stood there for ages before I started work, watching these gigantic Tonka Toys doing their bit. I was totally immersed in every aspect of everything that was going on.

Build milestones came thick and fast. The first delivery of steel. Steel work on the East Stand springing up. The vomitories appearing. The demolition of the small classrooms to make way for the cavernous West Stand. Witnessing each and every new chapter of the build, I just got more and more excited. How much more thrilling could it get?

Meanwhile, with the shell of the stadium taking shape, and hundreds of uploaded photos later, I now had an army of over one thousand interested stadium fans, eager for Friday to come to get their Falmer Fix.

All the stands taking shape nicely, and probably the highlight of the show, the placement of the arches. I arrived on site at 7.30am with my step-ladder, and waited for the first section to be lifted into place. It didn't happen until the afternoon, but I wasn't going to miss it, especially after escorting a part of it down from Hassocks on the A23. But that's another story!

Being given the privilege of the occasional visit inside to see the gleaming new lounges and the huge concourses taking shape, I felt that I was inspecting my new-build house. The seats started to go in, and the pitch got greener and greener. We were almost there.

Two and a half years and nearly 6,000 photos later, we are there. Our stadium is every bit as big, smart and classy as Dick and Martin said it would be – the perfect build in more ways than one. Completed on time and on budget. I can't believe how long it took to start with all the various delays, but once started, how quickly it was finished.

Most moments of joy last just a short while. The joy I've experienced since I snapped that digger nearly three years ago has been constant. I can't explain the ever-present uplifting feeling I've had during this time. The beauty here is that I know, without doubt, that our stadium, which I am so proud of, will be a joy for ever.

October 2008

ABOVE: The planning notice is posted on site.

Garry Mills

A new stadium... is it ever gonna happen? I'd asked myself that question over and over again, but when I saw the photo of that digger in the field, I began to realise that it was no longer a dream.

Things you didn't know about the Amex

2008

It took 10 years to get planning permission for the stadium.

ABOVE: Prior to commencement of works, it was a requirement of the planning permission that an archaeological dig took place.

Derek Chapman

I first met Kevin Underwood (Buckingham Director) at Stadium MK in early 2007 with Robert Comer and Ray Bloom. After 10 minutes I thought, "Here's a man I could do business with".

Things you didn't know about the Amex

912 days

It has taken 912 days to build the stadium.

ABOVE: 27th November 2008, stadium contract signed at Withdean Stadium our old home.

ABOVE: Neolithic spearheads unearthed.

Things you didn't know about the Amex

Team

Buckingham Group Contracting Limited were also the main contractors on Stadium MK.

ABOVE: First job by Buckingham was to securely fence the site.

ABOVE: Diggers for goalposts.

BUCKINGHAM
Future ho e of
Brighton & Albion.
errea

January 2009

ABOVE: Early days, early morning. Stripping top soil for construction of the coach park.

Bobby McGarrigle

It's hard to explain to someone who doesn't understand football why your heart skips a beat when you drive past a building site on the A27. We have made our dream come true for ourselves and the generations that will follow.

Things you didn't know about the Amex

Soil

All top soil was recycled on site for planting areas and on Village Way South.

ABOVE: Buckingham supervisors surveying the scene.

Things you didn't know about the Amex

Bus pass

The original Village Way was not wide enough to allow two buses to pass each other.

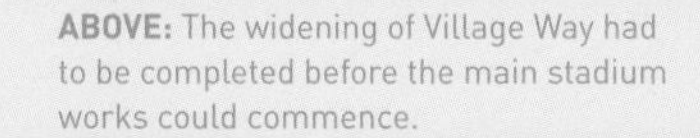

ABOVE: The widening of Village Way had to be completed before the main stadium works could commence.

BELL
B30D

March 2009

ABOVE: Buckingham were unable to close the road at anytime during construction, as access was required to the University and Leisure Centre.

Martin Perry

Putting the surplus excavated material on the field south of Village Way had two major benefits. Firstly, apart from avoiding major disruption on the local road network it saved the equivalent of 9 million footballs' worth of CO2 emissions. Secondly, re-levelling the field and increasing the depth of top soil resulted in the agricultural rating of the land being improved by one grade.

Things you didn't know about the Amex

£475,000

The nearest power supply big enough to handle the peak loads at the stadium was 3 miles away. A new cable was laid along the A270 as far as Stanmer Park and then fed underneath the railway and along the new footpath/cycle path serving the stadium. It cost over £475,000 to install.

Things you didn't know about the Amex

139,000m³

139,000m³ of chalk was dug out and moved to an adjacent field during stadium construction.

ABOVE: Village Way complete. Earth moving trucks move onto the site.

ABOVE: Hoarding denotes site boundary, as the University buildings remained in use until October 2009.

Ben Miller

I'm waiting for someone – probably a miserly NIMBY or a politician – to tap me on the shoulder, tell me it's been an elaborate hoax and tear it down.

Things you didn't know about the Amex

Big dig

The equivalent depth of a four storey house was dug out.

Jan Merritt

I mourned the loss of the Goldstone, travelling to Gillingham was woeful and Withdean inadequate, but seeing our new stadium at last coming to fruition was better than I had ever dreamed of in those dark days.

ABOVE: Such extensive excavation was required to ensure the stadium blended into the surrounding South Downs landscape.

ABOVE: Groundwork for the coach park drainage system is well under way.

Things you didn't know about the Amex

Carbon Footprint

By tipping soil on the field south of Village Way 22,000 return lorry journeys were saved on Sussex highways.

ABOVE: The average soil removal journey covered less than the length of two football pitches.

ABOVE: Foundations for the East Stand commence.

ABOVE: Fixing reinforcement cages.

Graham Willis

I've watched it rise out of the ground like a phoenix. Looking at it on webcam every day, driving past when possible, it looks magnificent, and I can't wait to see our team playing there. The atmosphere will be something home fans may almost have forgotten.

ABOVE: Health and Safety of paramount importance.

ABOVE: Work continues on steel reinforcement cages.

July 2009

ABOVE: The East Stand begins to take shape.

Things you didn’t know about the Amex

5,396

The number of Albion supporters the East Stand seats on a match day.

July 2009

Martin Perry

The planning process had taken so long many of our fans said they wouldn't believe the stadium was coming until they saw the diggers on site. When the diggers arrived some said, "We won't believe it until we see the steel going up". When the steel started going up some said, "We won't believe it until all the steelwork has been erected"! Some still think it's all a dream.

Sandra Chamberlain

Working opposite the Falmer site, I was able to witness the entire rise of our stadium. Having been wowed by what I could see from the outside, having now visited inside, I was awestruck by the sheer architectural classiness of it all really, and it's huge.

ABOVE: First steel erected on the East Stand.

ABOVE: Construction of in situ vomitories commences.

August 2009

ABOVE: East Stand superstructure progressing well.

Sharon Davey

Every day my fiancé would check the webcam and point out each new section. It was a joy to see his face light up as the stadium evolved. Thanks Dick and Tony for saving our club.

Things you didn't know about the Amex

Steel of approval

Subcontractors Watson Steel also worked on the 2012 Olympic Stadium, the Emirates Stadium, and the sliding roof at Wimbledon.

ABOVE: Step by step, the East Stand terrace work begins.

September 2009

ABOVE: Martin Perry surveys the site from pitch level.

Martin Perry

As the steel frame rose into the air the sheer scale of the building became obvious. You could see it from the A27!

ABOVE: Fans could check progress through one of the viewing portals.

Things you didn't know about the Amex

4,520 tonnes

4,520 tonnes of steel were used in the making of the stadium.

ABOVE: On 1st October 2009, the University of Brighton handed over their buildings and land so that demolition could commence, therefore giving possession of the whole site.

ABOVE: The arch was fabricated in Watson Steel's factory in the shadow of the Reebok Stadium, Bolton.

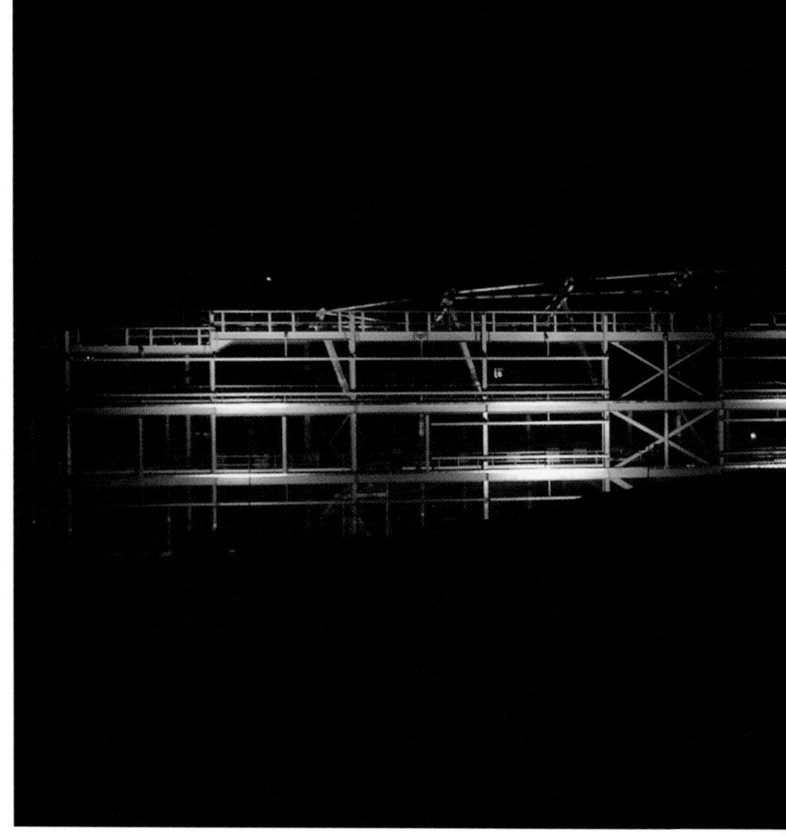

Tim Carder

Albion sought a new home on and off for more than a century – the Amex Stadium will be worth the wait! My thanks to everyone who made it happen.

ABOVE: Works carry on through the dark evenings after the clocks go back.

ABOVE: Electrical works begin inside the East Stand.

Things you didn't know about the Amex

Arch

The arch was delivered to site flat packed and then assembled in three sections.

ABOVE: The site looks a hive of activity in the late November sun.

ABOVE: Des Lynam and artist Mike Payne take a tour of the stadium. Mike created all the window artwork in Dick's Bar plus the banners behind the West Stand.

TCS
TCS
GREENHAM
GREENHAM
TCS

ABOVE: Steelwork surrounding one of the dogsheads.

December 2009

ABOVE: Lowering the capsule into its temporary home during construction.

Things you didn't know about the Amex

Time

The time capsule is in the North Stand concourse and on display for all.

Cliff Smith

Every single time I travel past the stadium site I get the exact same feeling as I used to when my dad took me to the Goldstone when I was little. That was 30 years ago. Waiting for the stadium to be completed, I've felt like a kid looking forwards to his presents on Christmas Day.

TOP: Local schools were invited to enter a competition to select the time capsule contents. The winners were Brighton & Hove School for Girls.

Clive Tinkler

Enjoy it, but never forget those last two years at the Goldstone. Sit ins, pitch invasions, games abandoned, fans arrested trying to save their club. Some games we had more police horses around the pitch than players on it. Just remember how we got here.

ABOVE: Peter Ward visits the site for his first glimpse of our new home.

ABOVE: Heavy lifting. The 600 ton capacity crane used to lift the arch was transported to the site from the Olympic Stadium in London.

Martin Perry

The bearings supporting each end of the arches were nicknamed 'dogsheads' as they reminded people of K9 (Doctor Who's dog).

ABOVE: The East Stand arch is lifted and lowered into place, during the stress testing period.

ABOVE: Scaffolding engulfs one of the dogsheads as it nears completion.

ABOVE: A Christmas picture postcard.

Martin Perry

Once the steelwork was erected the inside of the stadium began to take shape. In most stadiums the concourses are designed to cater for 46% of the supporters sitting in the stand they serve. At the Amex they are designed to cater for 56% of supporters, giving them more room to move around.

Mark Raven

Goldstone Ground RIP never forgotten, but this development at Falmer makes me proud to be a BHA supporter and now we can move forward!

Derek Chapman

It was one of the coldest winters I had ever known and I have lived in Brighton all my life. Most exposed were the steel erectors, luckily they all came from Bolton so it probably felt like mid-summer to them. If it hadn't been for Health and Safety reasons they would have had their shirts off.

ABOVE: Martin Perry takes shelter inside the East Stand concourse on a freezing January morning.

ABOVE: While the rest of the country takes a duvet day, workers paint sections of the arch in sub-zero conditions.

January 2010

Sam Hart

As I entered the site I could feel the butterflies in my stomach. I felt on top of the world, the first of my mates to actually go on site! You don't realise how amazing it really is until you're there in the flesh.

ABOVE: Snow hampers progress.

Norman Thomas

Having lived and worked in Brighton on the Amex Stadium for nearly two years, I feel very proud and humble to say I had a hand in building your magnificent new home. Your city is unique, your fans are unique and so now is your superb stadium.

Things you didn't know about the Amex

30,400m^2

The total building footprint of the stadium is 30,400m^2.

ABOVE: A separate contract funded by SEEDA was awarded for infrastructure works to provide a secondary access to the University of Sussex.

ABOVE: With the cold snap abating, it's full steam ahead with the construction of the lower ground floor West Stand commencing.

John Vallance

Is that really for us!? Little old Brighton? I still don't think it will really sink in until that first ball is kicked in anger. When it does, the trips to Gillingham, the torture of Edgar Street and the countless hours of protesting and campaigning will all finally make a bit more sense.

 ABOVE: Lifting the East Stand arch into place.

Martin Perry

Witnessing the arch being lifted into place for the first time was an emotional moment. I was reminded of the meetings in the architects' offices 10 years before when we had looked at various structural solutions for the stadium and the decision was taken to use the arch design. That dream had now become a reality.

February 2010

ABOVE: Blockwork begins and internal rooms start to take shape.

Beary Rolf

Paraphrasing another great builder, and to all those whose unflinching dedication and effort made this beautiful edifice possible "If you seek your monument, look around".

Things you didn't know about the Amex

High rise

The tallest point of the stadium is 35m high.

ABOVE: Steelwork continues at pace on the West Stand.

March 2010

ABOVE: Halfway home.

Things you didn't know about the Amex

6,000

The load on each end of the arch is 6,000 tonnes, equivalent to the force needed to stop an express train travelling at 60mph.

ABOVE: West Stand basement walls in temporary position.

Gil Waller

After the nomadic years at Gillingham, and then Withdean, I monitored the photos on the websites to witness the growing magnificence of Falmer each week. It was sinking in. It's happening.

Things you didn't know about the Amex

Cosy

Insulated cladding helped to achieve the accolade of being the most eco-friendly stadium in the country.

ABOVE: In excess of 1,000 cladding panels slot into place like a giant jigsaw.

ABOVE: Fabricating the lighting gantries before being lifted into position.

Stewart Teeder

As the Amex Stadium goes up it provides the focal point of a new home but it is much, much more. It is the arena for our future generations. It will have unrivalled atmosphere, holding in all of the noise from every single fan with a voice that can be heard. It will bring pride to our city and jobs and opportunities for its citizens. It is our ground, our home where over 20,000 people can now feel they belong. I will look forward to going to the Amex with my dad and my son knowing that my family has a great future to look forward to supporting the club.

ABOVE: Martin Perry uses a coffee cup to mark the centre spot for John Prescott.

Things you didn't know about the Amex

Tunnelvision

It is 39m from the home dressing room to pitchside.

Martin Perry

During the 2010 election campaign John Prescott let us know he was visiting Brighton. He arrived in his battle bus complete with loudspeakers and made a grand entrance. Having been so involved in the planning process and sharing our vision for what the stadium would do for the club and the community he was thrilled to see that it was actually coming to fruition. He left chanting "Seagulls" over the loud speaker'.

Neil Stapley

Every time the Albion were at home, we drove over from Hastings to Withdean, making a point of stopping off at Falmer en route to peer through the holes in the fence. When we finally got inside for the Sussex Senior Cup Final, there wasn't a dry eye amongst us. when Good Old Sussex by the Sea blared out.

TOP: A busy site seen from the East Stand.

MIDDLE: First sight of the fully clad East Stand.

BOTTOM: Strongbacks support the tunnel walls in a temporary condition.

Things you didn't know about the Amex

100 steps

There are 100 steps from the ground floor to the upper concourse in the West Stand.

ABOVE: Construction worker surveying the site from the top tier of the West Stand.

Margaret Simmonds

All those years of campaigning, petitioning, leafleting and arguing with people who told me that the site wasn't suitable had finally ended and the result of all the hard work was clearly visible. Wonderful.

ABOVE: Glaziers go to great panes to install glass in the East Stand.

ABOVE: Surveyor positioning the formwork for the South Stand terracing.

May 2010

Martin Perry

The huge West Stand was now beginning to take shape. Vast spaces that were to become the hospitality suites appeared almost overnight and we began to see for the first time the fabulous views from the upper concourses.

ABOVE: The West Stand stairwells take shape.

ABOVE: A section of pre-cast terracing is lifted into place on the top tier.

ABOVE: Metal decking awaiting a concrete topping to the second floor of the West Stand.

Things you didn't know about the Amex

32 flights

The impressive West Stand houses 32 flights of stairs.

May 2010

ABOVE: 12 months until completion.
The West Stand arch is assembled
and ready to be hoisted high.

ABOVE: Workers oversee the lifting of another section of terracing.

ABOVE: Powerfloat polishing the surface of the West Stand floor to a high quality finish.

Things you didn't know about the Amex

64,900

64,900 tonnes of locally supplied concrete were used in the stadium construction process.

April 2010

ABOVE: Structure going up in the Downs.

David Swaffield

I won't be happy until I'm sat in my seat, at our beautiful new home. The battle is over. Job done. Looking back, the Goldstone now seems a lifetime away. She is recalled now as an old woman who knew how to party in her day.

ABOVE: Water sprayed on dusty surfaces to keep the site clean.

ABOVE: Now where does this bracket go?

ABOVE: Sparks fly as a welder gets to work on a section of gas piping in the West Stand.

Things you didn't know about the Amex

21,202

There are 21,202 metres of pipe work in the stadium.

Martin Perry

The architects had now turned their attention to the interior design and finishes in the stadium. The brief was to create top quality hospitality suites for corporate guests on a match day and a brand new conferencing and banqueting facility in the South East of England for non-match day use. The revenues from non-match day use of the stadium are vital to the success of the club.

ABOVE : Samples of hospitality lounge fabric furnishings on display at the Marketing Suite.

TOP LEFT: Right here, right now. Fatboy Slim visits the site.

TOP RIGHT: All is revealed. The stadium is now called the American Express Community Stadium.

BOTTOM LEFT: Marketing Suite onsite opens for sales of 1901 Club.

BOTTOM RIGHT: Naming rights day, a huge step in the history of the stadium.

ABOVE: At its busiest over 300 people worked on the stadium construction.

WELDEX

ABOVE: Taking a break.

TOP: Checking position of staircase. **BOTTOM**: Setting out the arch.

June 2010

ABOVE: The view from the North Stand showing both arches in situ.

Things you didn't know about the Amex

25 years

The paint used is designed to protect the steel for a quarter of a century.

Derek Chapman

I am never happier than when there are lots of big cranes on the site. They are serious boys' toys.

Ray McSweeney

As soon as the contractors started to dig and remove the chalk from the site, I realised this was actually it. It had started. All the frustration of the last 10 years was going to come to an end. The dream was coming true.

ABOVE: Workers paint sections of the roof joists.

ABOVE: Tim Dudding fuels the webcam battery cells ensuring fans are kept updated.

June 2010

Ayhan Suleyman

Falmer, for me and my son, will be the start of an amazing new era for the club which will serve its deserving fans well for generations to come. As we get older, I look forward to sharing many tense moments, happy moments and sad moments with my son in the real theatre of dreams.

ABOVE: Lifting rafters into place.

July 2010

Martin Perry

With the arches in place and the structure nearing completion there was huge interest being generated from both the fans and people working for the club. We arranged tours for the players and staff so they could both get a feel and be inspired by what was coming.

ABOVE: Gully's Girls (and Gully) have their own changing room in the West Stand.

ABOVE: Purlins on which the roof sheeting is fixed, are being placed into position.

ABOVE: Cladding commences to West Stand and steelwork to infill corners.

ABOVE: The curves of the roof as they complement the surrounding hillside.

Things you didn't know about the Amex

Farmer 4 all

Following the re-profiling of land south of Village Way it will take five years for it to be restored to full agricultural use.

ABOVE: Trusses have been removed and the roof and arches are now self-supporting.

Derek Chapman

Originally the roof at both ends of the stadium was going to be top soiled and grassed. It would have been impossible to cut grass on a 75 degree slope, four storeys in the air! Luckily common sense prevailed.

Jimmy Beeney

Seeing the stadium for the first time actually brought tears to my eyes. After all our years of struggle and pain, that sight erased many of those bad memories.

TOP LEFT: Steelwork to corner progressing to form the fully enclosed bowl.

TOP RIGHT: East Stand exterior nears completion.

ABOVE: Roofing above the away end takes shape.

Martin Perry

The North Stand has a long tradition particularly for Albion supporters, many of whom have fond memories of standing behind the goal at the Goldstone. It was now beginning to take shape.

ABOVE: A view of the interior of the North Stand concourse.

ABOVE: The Club Shop in its early form.

ABOVE: Cutting edge. Final adjustments to steelwork.

September 2010

ABOVE: The first TV camera allowed inside the stadium to film progress.

Things you didn't know about the Amex

147m

The train station is 147m from the nearest entrance to the stadium.

ABOVE: Middle section of the new footbridge across the railway tracks is lifted into place.

Martin Perry

Walking out from the players' tunnel for the first time was awesome. It stirred up a vision of the battles on the pitch to come.

Things you didn't know about the Amex

783,588

783,588 metres of cable have been installed in the building which equals 487 miles, further than the distance between Brighton and Glasgow.

ABOVE: Paul and Karen Goldsmith from IT First view their new executive box.

ABOVE: Tommy Elphick, Elliott Bennett and Adam El-Abd given a tour of the stadium.

TCS
TCS

 ABOVE: Tiling the home team shower room.

Things you didn't know about the Amex

Early bath

There are 10 showers in the home team changing room.

Graham Hollebon

Proud to be Albion, proud to be Sussex, proud of the part I played in the fight to win our beautiful new home. When I saw this I finally believed that at long last we were going to have a proper ground again – somewhere we could call home!

ABOVE: Stephen Grant shouts "Seagulls" for the first time.

ABOVE: Glazed curtain wall installation under way.

Things you didn't know about the Amex

Beer

Harveys and Dark Star brewers' ales will be on sale at all kiosks and bars in the stadium.

ABOVE: Deal signed with Harveys to provide real ale in the stadium bars.

Things you didn't know about the Amex

2,600

2,600 match day premier seats (known as 1901 Club) have been sold.

TOP: Season ticket office opens for business.

MIDDLE: Home team changing room under construction.

BOTTOM: SEEDA highway works near completion.

TOP: Suspended from the West Stand arch. This workman adds paintwork.

BOTTOM: A view of the site progress taken from the top tier of the West Stand.

December 2010

ABOVE: Stadium concourse artists view their blank canvas for the first time.

Martin Perry

The South East England Development Agency (SEEDA) saw the benefits the stadium would bring in terms of opportunities for education, skills training and jobs. To assist the development they funded a new junction that not only opened up access to the stadium but also improved the access to the University of Sussex, a new regional archive and the new Academy being built on the site of the former Falmer High School.

TOP: Glowing in the winter sun.

BOTTOM: Fan made statement on the hoardings.

BOTTOM: SEEDA funded flyover works complete. Leader of Brighton City Council, Mary Mears, officially opens the interchange.

ABOVE: During one of the coldest winters in years work continues.

January 2011

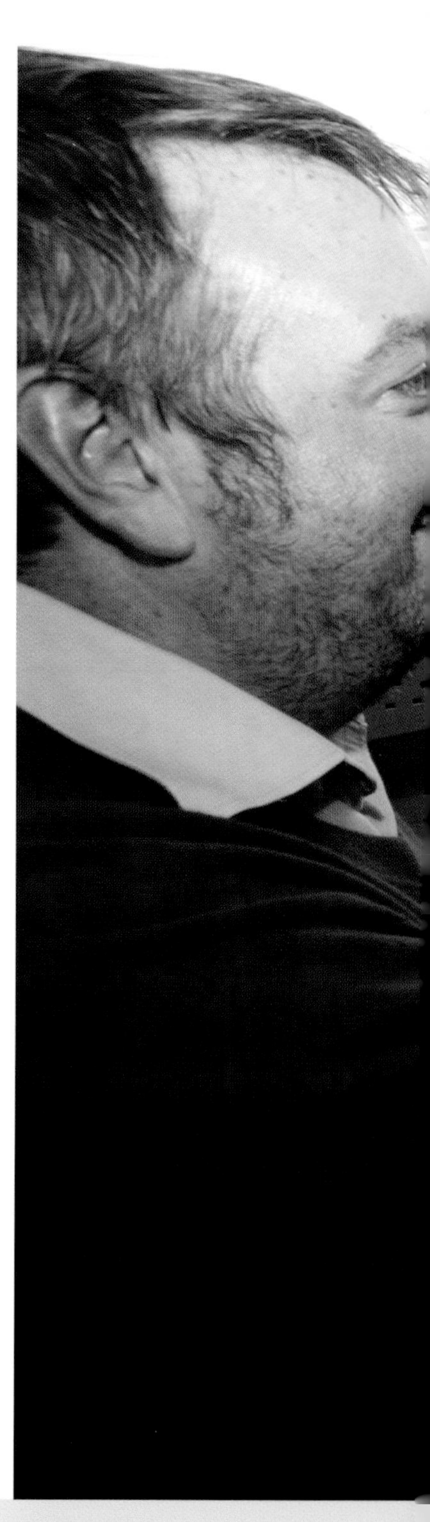

Things you didn't know about the Amex

Smart cards

The season tickets are smart cards and act as "pre-pay" cards as well as access control.

ABOVE: Additional staff join the team to help meet demand for season tickets.

ABOVE: Paul Samrah and John Baine purchase the first two season tickets.

RUFFIANS

ABOVE: Installation of undersoil drainage system to the pitch.

Things you didn't know about the Amex

Big'uns

The pitch dimensions are the largest allowed. It is the same size as Wembley.

Martin Perry

The pitch is made up of a series of levels, a drainage layer, lower root zone, upper root zone and growing medium. The top surface is a mix of top soil, fibre and elastic which simulates the resilience of a newly grown pitch to aid grass recovery and reduce the wear on players' joints. It is one of the most technologically advanced pitches in the country and shortly after opening got a five star rating from an independent pitch specialist.

ABOVE: Scaffolding is erected to construct the curved ceiling in the Lower Platinum Lounge.

ABOVE: Seat brackets are installed on the East Stand terrace.

Bob Wadey

As a Goldstone regular it broke my heart when the ground was sold, although a magnificent phoenix has arisen from the flames.

ABOVE: Catering equipment installation commences in the concourse kiosks.

ABOVE: Closing off the external façade of the South West corner.

ABOVE: Seagull's eye view.

Paul Goldsmith

It was a very surreal experience, walking into our box for the first time. I always hoped that one day we would get a new home to watch our team, and my dreams have become a reality after 13 long years. How special is that?

ABOVE: From the air the extent of the SEEDA works can be seen.

ABOVE: Derek Chapman sets off on another recon mission.

Things you didn't know about the Amex

Albion pies

Albion pies are all made in-house and served at kiosks and hospita

ABOVE: Catering team wait in anticipation for the verdict from Albion director Derek Chapman.

Derek Chapman

One of the greatest honours in my life has to be the fact that I chose the stadium pies, and I am sure everyone will agree they are Premiership quality.

ABOVE: Interior of concourse kiosks nearing completion..

Things you didn't know about the Amex

Access

Every bar has disabled access.

TOP: External nosing providing the stadium with its unique roof lines.

BOTTOM: Main external concourse steps and access ramp for our disabled supporters.

ABOVE: One fan lost in contemplation.

AMEX

ABOVE: Subsoil and top soil being laid by laser guided tractor.

Things you didn't know about the Amex

Maintenance

The grass is cut between five and seven times a week.

Sarah Watts

I remember being very excited when Martin Perry took us round in September 2010. He took us up into the top tier of the West Stand and told us that we couldn't look until he had us positioned just so. When we were allowed to look my first thought was....WOW!

ABOVE: Each lorry load of soil delivered is analysed in the laboratory for compliance with specification.

Martin Perry

With the roof and the cladding completed we could now see how the stadium was imitating the roll of the Downs. It fitted perfectly.

Things you didn't know about the Amex

Spotlight

The floodlights are designed to light the pitch to an average level of 800 lux.

ABOVE: West Stand cladding gleaming in the sunlight.

ABOVE: Seating rails fixed in the East Stand ready to receive seats.

ABOVE: The wrapping comes off.

Things you didn't know about the Amex

On programme

The stadium has 210 TV screens.

 ABOVE: Directors take a tour of the new stadium.

ABOVE: Chairman Tony Bloom pleased with progress on site.

ABOVE: An aerial view of the completed roofscape photographed from Derek Chapman's helicopter.

Things you didn't know about the Amex

6th August

The first League football match at the Amex was held on 6th August 2011 against Doncaster Rovers, the last team that the Albion played at the Goldstone Ground in 1997.

ABOVE: Photographer Paul Hazlewood gets a seagull's eye view.

ABOVE: On the right track. The main structure nears completion on the railway footbridge at Falmer Station.

Things you didn't know about the Amex

25,000

25,000 travel passes were printed for the first season at the new stadium.

Martin Perry

The interiors of the hospitality suites were designed to reflect the roll of the South Downs, the waves of the sea and the seagulls flying.

ABOVE: The ceiling in the Upper Platinum Lounge is being installed.

Things you didn't know about the Amex

1,100

1,100 trees have been planted at the stadium site.

Stuart James

When I looked through one of the little peep-holes in the blue hoarding, I could clearly see the disabled viewing platform being constructed in the corner. I then realised that myself and my two disabled children would be able to watch the Albion with a superb view in the utmost comfort, and in the dry.

TOP: Landscaping is well under way along Village Way.

BOTTOM: The drainage layer is levelled and ready.

ABOVE: The first catering contracts are discussed in the East Stand concourse.

TCS
TCS
TCS

April 2011

 ABOVE: A tractor levelling out the pitch prior to seeding.

ABOVE: Seating in the West Stand upper tier being fitted into place.

Things you didn't know about the Amex

Comfy

The standard seats in the Amex are the same as the VIP seats in the Olympic Stadium being built in London.

Martin Perry

Every seat in the stadium is padded. The fact that the seats we have used in the general admission areas are the same as the VIP seats in the Olympic stadium just shows we think that every single one of our supporters is a VIP.

ABOVE: Once installed seats are covered to protect them from the elements prior to the first match.

TOP LEFT: Final levelling of pitch prior to seeding.

TOP RIGHT: Artificial turf to touchline being laid.

BOTTOM LEFT: There are seven different types of grass seed in the mix.

BOTTOM RIGHT: Seed being mechanically distributed onto the pitch.

ABOVE: It's in the bag. Grass seed unloaded by groundsman.

GRASS SEED
Kestrel

 ABOVE: Testing of external lighting.

Things you didn't know about the Amex

Lights off

There are 7,147 light fittings which switch off automatically if there is no movement after 30 minutes in each room.

John Cowen

Viewed from beneath, that soaring roof dips and twists around the site like some improbable fairground ride, seducing the punter with the promise of long-denied pleasures hidden within. So perfectly Brighton.

ABOVE: Complexity of steelwork connections illuminated.

Things you didn't know about the Amex

32,425

32,425 paving slabs were used to make the stadium concourse.

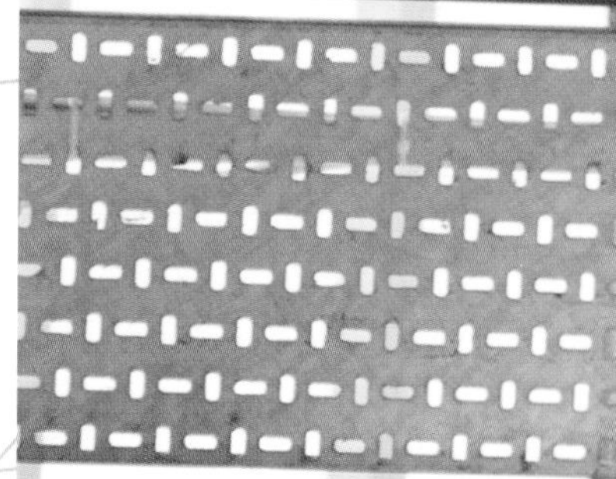

 ABOVE: Paving the way to success.

ABOVE: Specialist trained abseiler tidies up paintwork.

PETZL

Nick Szczepanik

I'm a Roedean Cafe regular, and somehow the way home usually seems to take me over the Falmer Road. When the arch arrived, it began to hit home how amazing the stadium was going to be.

ABOVE: Casting the final external concrete walls.

ABOVE: Bar being installed in the West Stand.

Things you didn't know about the Amex

Press gang

There are 52 press seats for journalists in the stadium.

Martin Perry

Only a month to go. Internally areas were being finished off. Externally the concourses, roads and landscaping were taking shape.

ABOVE: Work commences on the press area in the West Stand.

ABOVE: Marking the final countdown.

ABOVE: Buckingham safety manager reflecting on the fact that there were no serious injuries on site.

Things you didn't know about the Amex

15 cameras

There are 15 cameras filming every game from different locations.

Martin Perry

The safety of our supporters is paramount. Over the years huge lessons have been learned and the design of the stadium reflects the very latest standards in safety. The CCTV, public address and emergency systems were all put in the design and specification provided by our Head of Operations Richard Hebberd and rigorously tested before supporters were allowed in the stadium.

TOP: The control room behind the North Stand.

MIDDLE: Inside view taken from the location of the webcam.

BOTTOM: 24/7. The webcam records every moment.

Derek Chapman

To form the parabolic curve to the terracing every section of terrace is built at a different height. This makes it more complicated to build but provides optimum viewing angles for supporters.

ABOVE: Workmen make use of the lifts as soon as they are installed.

ABOVE: Concourse artist adds finishing touches to painting of the stadium.

ABOVE: Painting the white nosing on the steps accentuates the parabolic curve to the West Stand lower tier.

 ABOVE: Tunnel interior finishing well under way.

Things you didn't know about the Amex

$540m^2$

The Club Shop in the North Stand is $540m^2$.

Elizabeth Finn

When I saw the white metal work being put in place at the top of the East Stand, I got excited believing this to be the arch just for the upper tier, which would hopefully arrive later. Then the huge West Stand arch appeared, hovering above, thirty feet higher.

ABOVE: Dick's Bar and Club Shop construction.

ABOVE: A month to go and seating installation is well under wway.

ABOVE: Promoted. Banner erected to celebrate promotion to the Championship.

Martin Perry

The 2010/2011 season was drawing to a close. We had been promoted with four matches still to play. We now knew that we would be playing Championship football in our new home. You couldn't write the script. Fairy tales do come true.

ABOVE: Floodlight testing viewed from above and at ground level.

Things you didn't know about the Amex

25–30mm

The grass is always cut to 25–30mm.

Brett Mendoza

I was 16 when we left the Goldstone. This was my 30th birthday. It's truly beautiful - never has a building site ever been so arousing!

Martin Perry

The most important part of the whole stadium is the pitch. Having chosen a very advanced specification we had to make sure that it was laid properly and then maintained to ensure that it was ready for the first events in July 2011. Steve Winterburn our Head Groundsman scrupulously supervised the whole process.

ABOVE: First cut of grass by pitch contractor.

ABOVE: Sparkling stadium.

ABOVE: Pitch being irrigated four times a day as part of the bedding process.

Things you didn't know about the Amex

45,000

[illegible] tank that stores the water for the pitch [illegible] system can hold 45,000 litres.

Things you didn't know about the Amex

Park and ride

The stadium is served by three park and ride sites.

Jeremy Short

What most struck me was the awesome sight of the three-tiered West Stand dominating the skyline. I realised then that the Albion were going to have a stadium that would inspire all fans and players.

ABOVE: Archaeological works to Bennetts Field.

BUCKINGHAM
RAMP
10

TOP: West Stand reception glazing completed.

BOTTOM: Bar installation. West Stand Lower Gold North.

ABOVE: Light fittings installed in Club Shop.

TOP: CCTV installation to control room.

BOTTOM: Concrete thrustblock in North Stand second floor.

ABOVE: Scaffolding removed revealing impressive new ceiling.

Things you didn't know about the Amex

Ice bath

There is an ice bath and a Jacuzzi in the changing rooms that can seat three players in each.

Things you didn't know about the Amex

7.5 by 11m

The players' warm-up room has a 4G artificial pitch measuring 7.5m by 11m.

Things you didn't know about the Amex

Staffing

There are 91 club staff based in the North Stand.

ABOVE: Martin Perry and Kevin Underwood (Buckingham Director) celebrate the official handing over of the stadium on 31st May 2011 – the date originally agreed.

Things you didn't know about the Amex

500mm

Stadium seats are 500mm wide.

Martin Perry

In the contract we signed in November 2008 the completion date was 31st May 2011. On the due day Buckingham handed us the keys, or to be more precise a little plastic card which opened all the doors. What an achievement, the stadium handed over on time and within its original budget.

ABOVE: The visitors' viewing platform, in place for almost two and a half years, is finally removed.

June 2011

Sue Wright

The first time I drove down Falmer Road from Woodingdean and saw the view of our stadium over the brow of the hill, it gave me goose bumps!

ABOVE: Everybody's favourite screensaver.

June 2011

ABOVE: Workers laying the first batch of heritage stones in front of the West Stand reception.

Things you didn't know about the Amex

All white

There are 450 white seats in the stadium.

ABOVE: The fisheye view of the stadium interior showing huge progress.

ABOVE: The very first directors' meeting to be held in the boardroom.

ABOVE: Head Groundsman Steve Winterburn pictured with one of his many new toys.

BLEC
MULTI-SEEDER 2

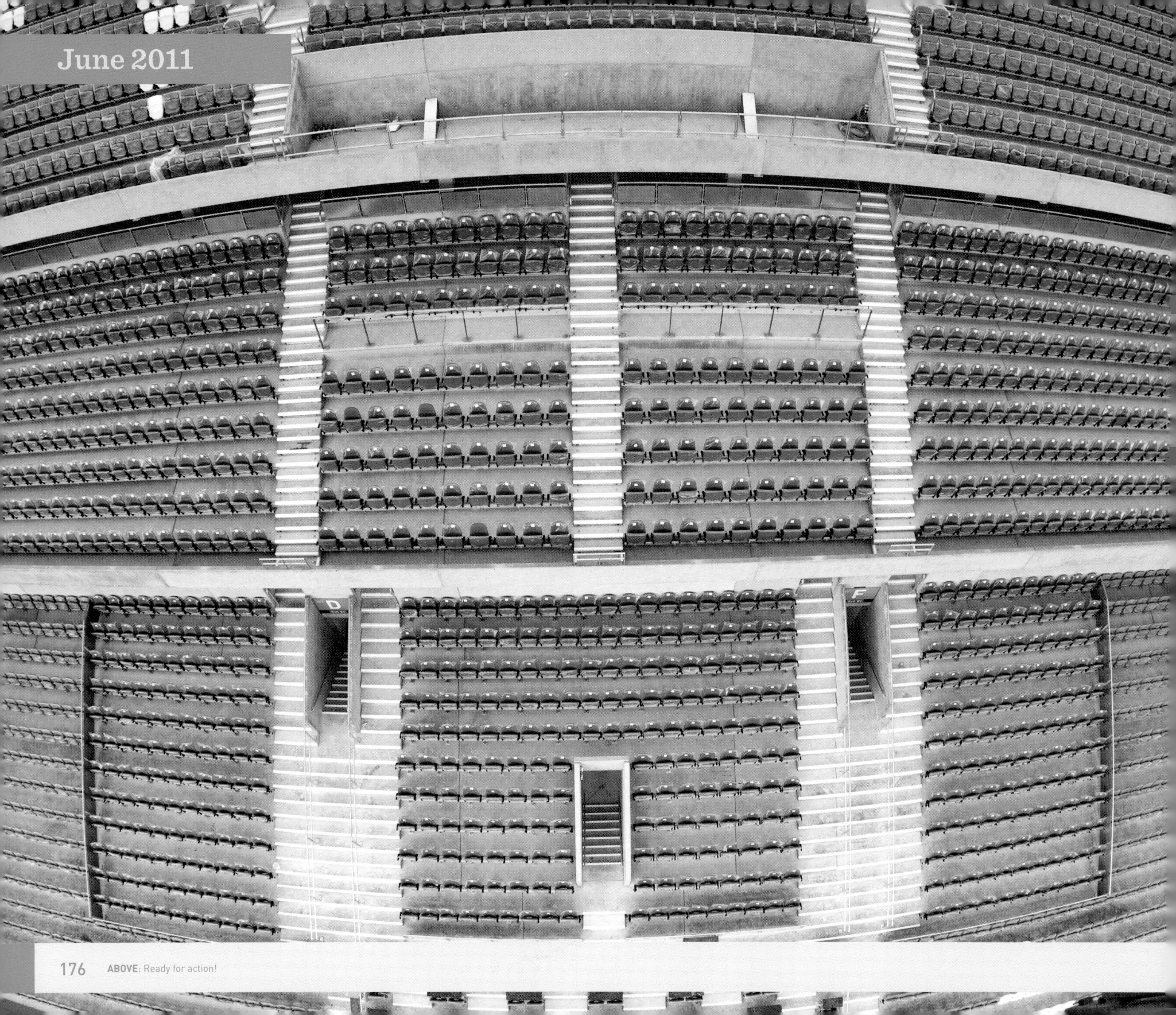

 ABOVE: Ready for action!

Things you didn't know about the Amex

Journalists

Sports journalists have their own private bar at the Amex.

Things you didn't know about the Amex

Driving seat

There are 34 seats in the dugout, 17 on each side.

Adrian Ayling

I'm just amazed at the sheer scale, sitting up here in the West Stand. Champions League here we come?

ABOVE: A view of the tunnel area prior to dugout seats being installed.

Martin Perry

The pitch was marked out for the very first time. It was only then that the sheer size of it became obvious. The Football League came down to check that we complied with their ground criteria. They measured the pitch, the changing rooms and the referee's facilities. For the first time in 12 years we fully complied with their regulations. They went away happy!

Things you didn't know about the Amex

Concerts

The Amex has permission to run two concerts per year

TOP LEFT: Pitch marking for the very first time.

TOP RIGHT: Ground staff building the goals.

BOTTOM LEFT: Dugout seating installed complete with covers.

BOTTOM RIGHT: You have been warned!

ABOVE: Undercoat to the striking blue tarmac surround being installed.

 ABOVE: Finishing touches to backlit signage.

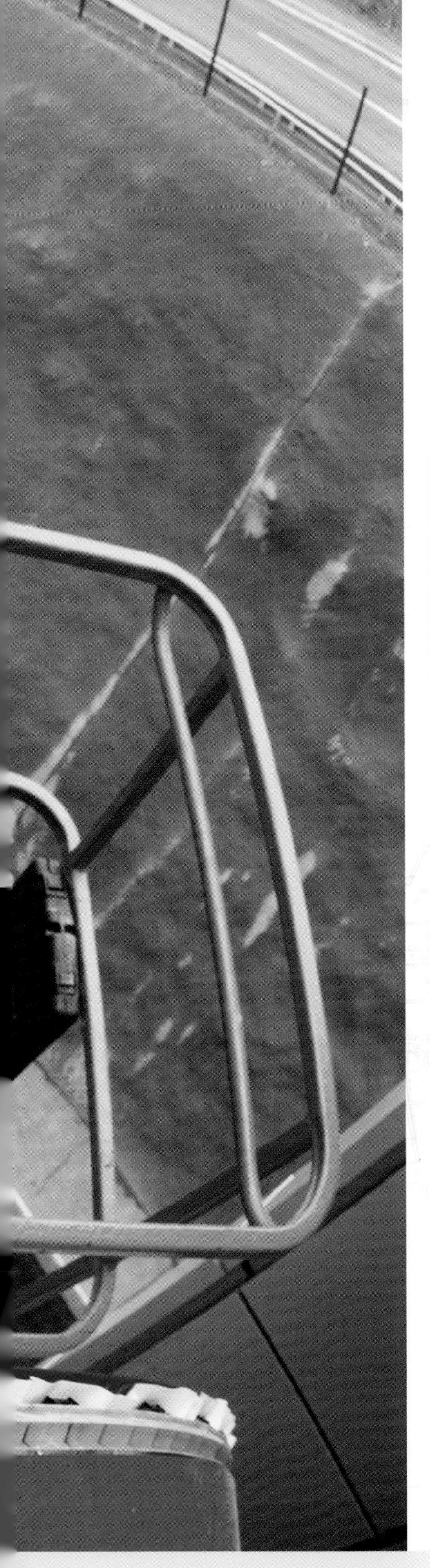

Martin Perry

We placed the signage package with a local firm, Icon Graffiti. It included the new club logo, the American Express Community Stadium logo and all the way-finding signage. It took over three months to install all the signs.

Things you didn't know about the Amex

Cycles

There are 234 cycle racks at the stadium.

ABOVE: New club crest emblem is revealed.

ABOVE: The impressive shop totem is illuminated at night.

Things you didn't know about the Amex

Rolling

The stadium design concept is based on the roll of the South Downs.

ABOVE: A fisheye view of the tunnel and dugout from the pitch.

ABOVE: An aerial view of the entire foot print showing Bennetts Field carpark under construction.

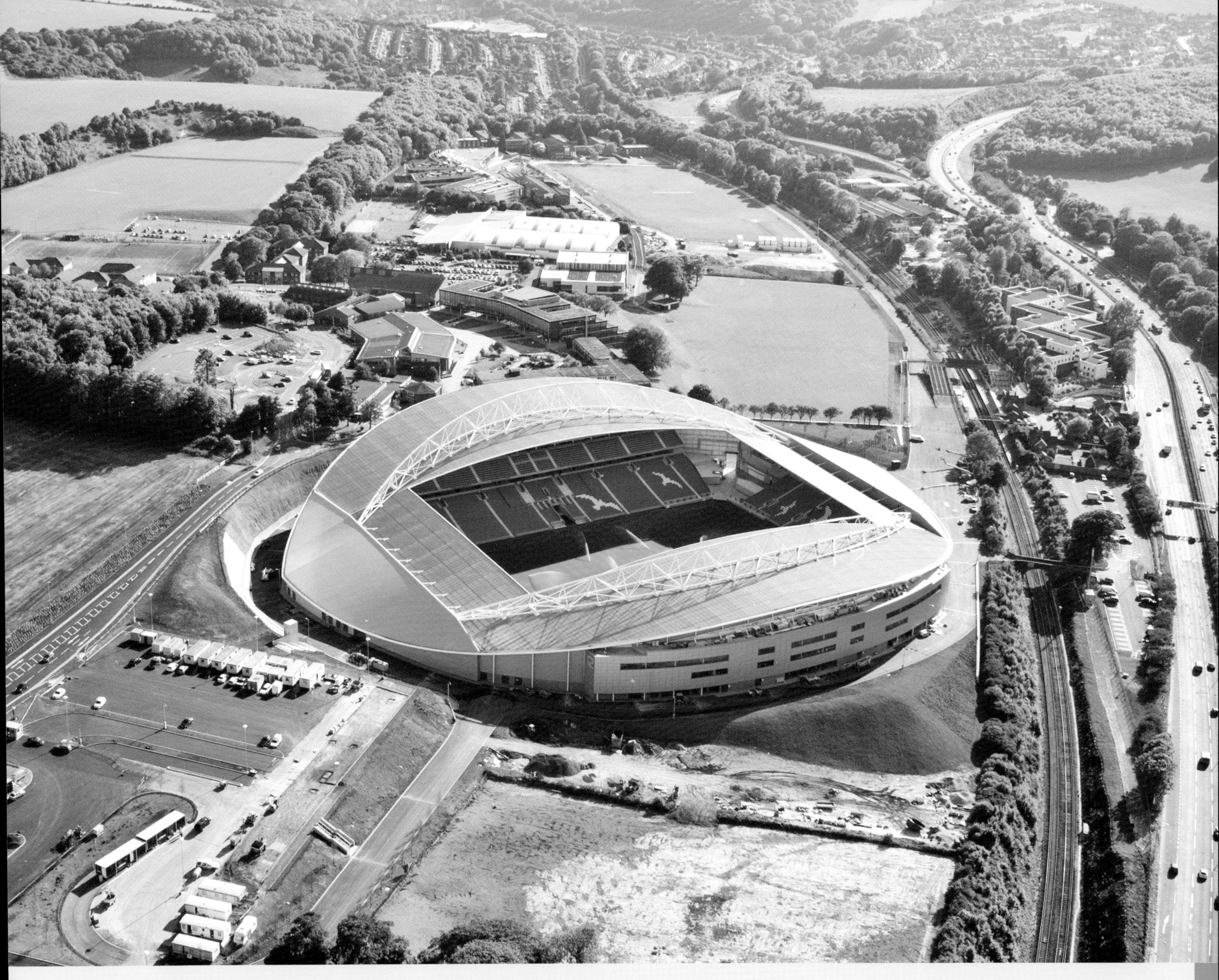

ABOVE: Pitch handover to the grounds maintenance team took place on 23rd June 2011.

Martin Perry

The race was now on to install nearly £3 million worth of furniture, fittings and equipment. We had to get the stadium ready for the first ramp up event due to be held on 16th July 2011.

Things you didn't know about the Amex

Sown

The pitch has been sown, not turfed.

ABOVE: Goals in position.

ABOVE: Access equipment installed at turnstiles ready for first paying customers.

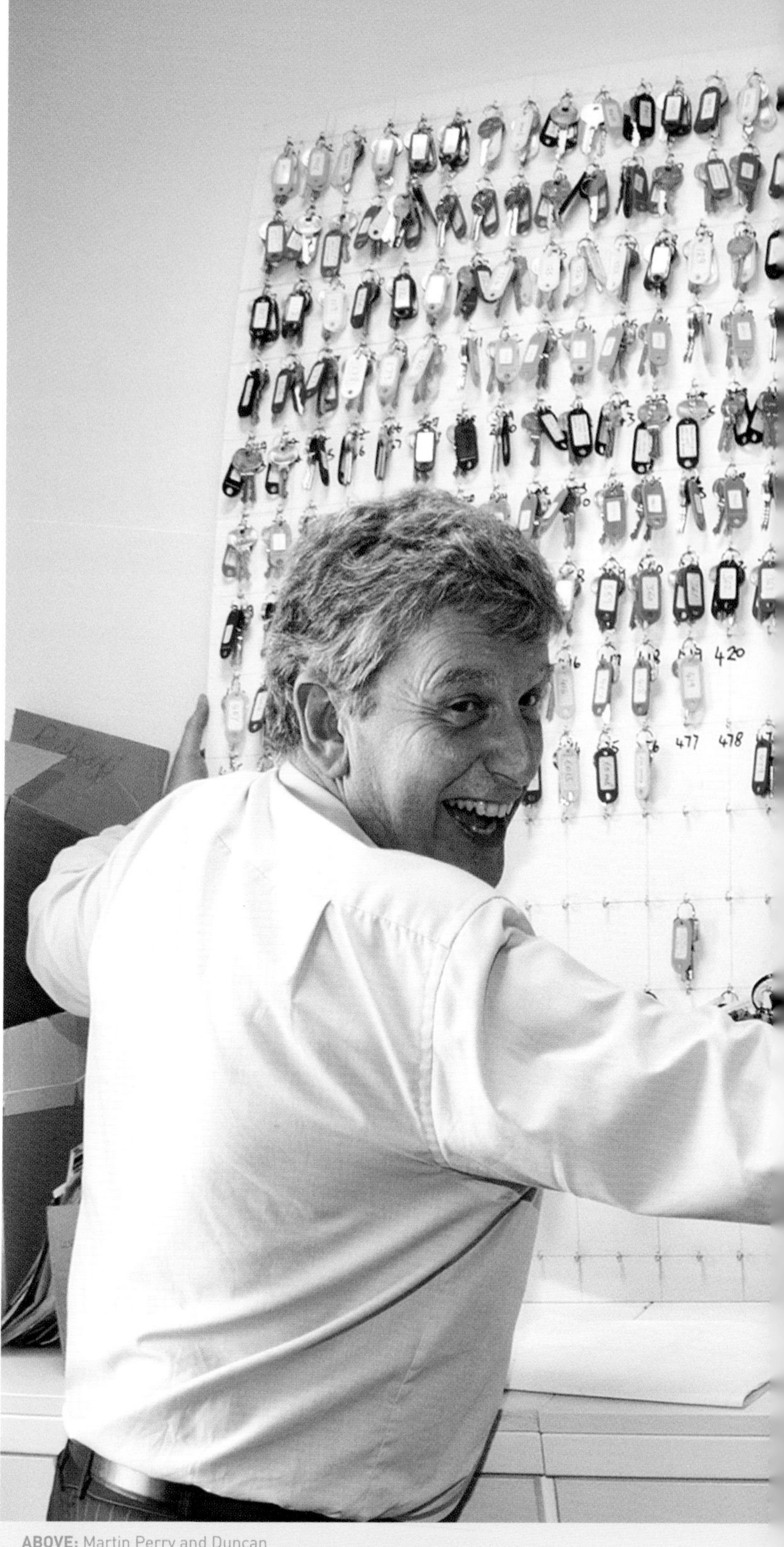

TOP: Bringing home the crown jewels.

BOTTOM: Boardroom furniture awaiting the first game.

ABOVE: Martin Perry and Duncan Halliday (Buckingham Project Manager) holding the key to success.

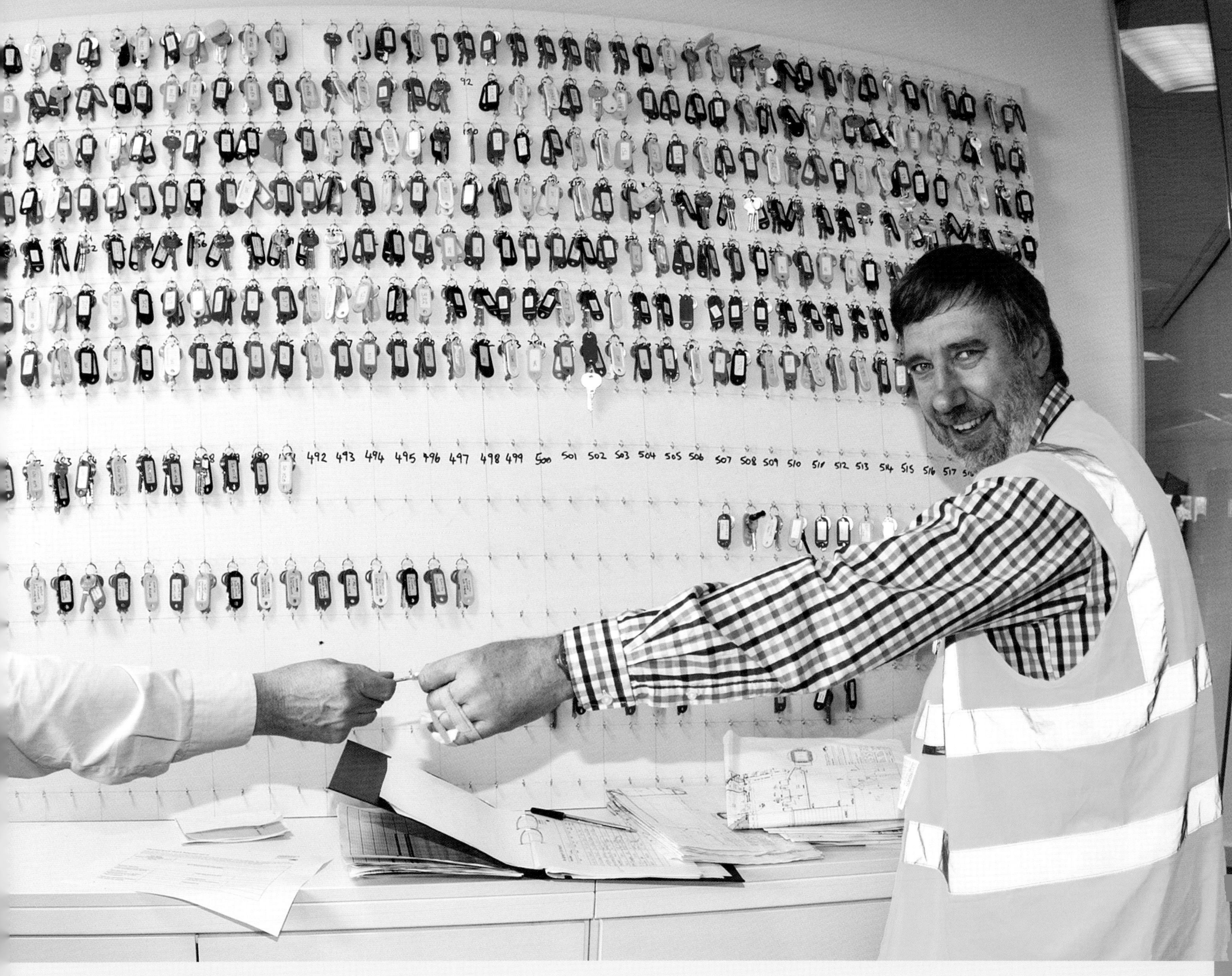
492 493 494 495 496 497 498 499 500 501 502 503 504 505 506 507 508 509 510 511 512 513 514 515 516 517

Things you didn't know about the Amex

Tours

Stadium tours include the changing rooms.

ABOVE: Away changing room.

ABOVE: Home changing room.
With no corners to hide in.

ABOVE: Individual LED blocks fitted into giant screens.

Things you didn't know about the Amex

Giant screens

The giant screens are the same as those used by the New England Patriots American football team in the Gillette Stadium in Foxborough, Massachusetts, USA.

ABOVE: Once the screen is installed the final seats can be completed.

Things you didn't know about the Amex

6,000

The number of pint glasses ordered for the stadium.

ABOVE: Dick's Bar is ready to open.

ABOVE: Some of the 138 tills installed around the stadium.

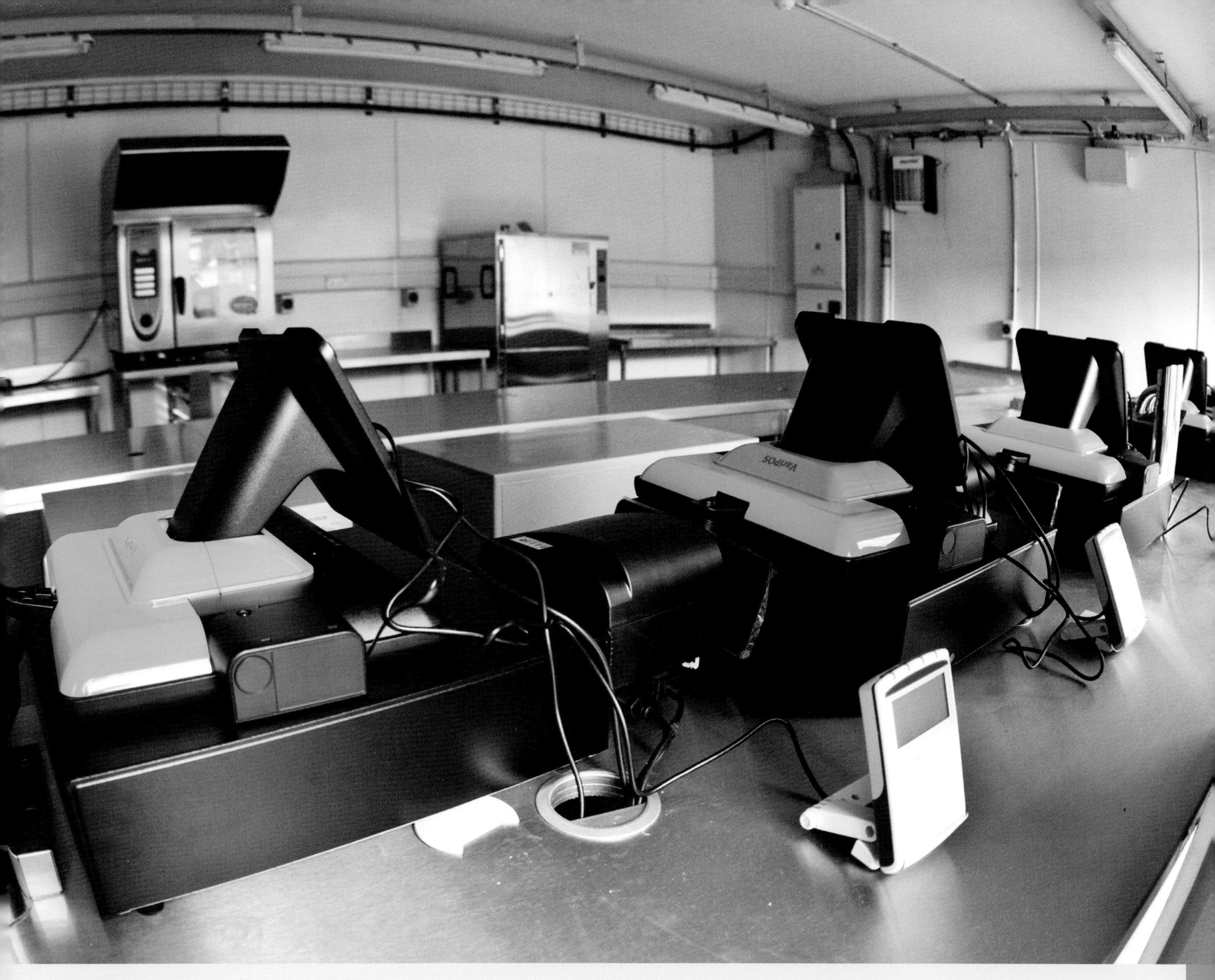
VariPOS

Andy Heryet

The marches – which encompassed participants from all sections of society – were instrumental in conveying the right message to the right audience; be that John Prescott and the ruling Parliamentary party, those minded to oppose the development, or the general Sussex public; that this stadium had mass community appeal and was not just something designed to satisfy a niche interest group.

ABOVE: Fitting the handrail for the disabled ramp.

ABOVE: Assembling the furniture.

ABOVE: The carpet is down and the furniture delivered in the Bupa Lounge.

Things you didn't know about the Amex

Price range

£2 million has been spent on equipment for the kitchens.

ABOVE: One of the seven kitchens inside the West Stand.

ABOVE: Diggers replaced by goalposts.

Exit

ABOVE: External signage being fitted alongside the legends banners.

ABOVE: Advertising boards being fitted into place.

Education
Amex
Stadium

ABOVE: The Bupa Lounge hosting its first major event.

Things you didn't know about the Amex

300 tables

There are 300 tables to lay each match.

Martin Perry

At Withdean we had a maximum number of 153 corporate guests on a match day. At the Amex we now cater for 2,600 corporate guests.

ABOVE: The Profile Lounge laid up ready for action.

ABOVE: The East Stand Brasserie also under starter's orders.

 ABOVE: Midnight sun.

Things you didn't know about the Amex

Grow

In total there are five sets of grow lights at the Amex, one of which was from Withdean.

ABOVE: Lighting in the club office reception area in the North Stand.

Things you didn't know about the Amex

£250m

The Amex forms part of a total of £250 million worth of building work in the Falmer area.

ABOVE: A seagull inspects the stadium.

ABOVE: Finishing touches to the pitch surround areas are applied with precision.

Helen Burchell

To see the seats going in... that's my seat! This is really going to happen, our shiny new future. Amazing feeling.

Derek Chapman

During Match of the Day I spent most of my time looking at the stadiums rather than watching the games. The idea for the blue paint around the perimeter of the pitch came from Manchester City.

Things you didn't know about the Amex

Weddings

The Amex has been licensed to host weddings at the stadium.

ABOVE: The manager's office in the first team restricted access zone.

ABOVE:The staff offices behind the North Stand terrace.

ABOVE: Official opening of the bridge across the railway. Club employee Kelly Eveson cuts the tape on 7th July 2011 watched by Network Rail, Southern Railways, Buckingham and club staff.

Things you didn't know about the Amex

Artists

Each indoor concourse is decorated with local artists' work, with a different theme in each concourse.

Derek Chapman

When I first became involved in the construction of the stadium in early 2007 I foresaw that the biggest problem would be with reaching agreement and gaining permissions from Network Rail. I wasn't wrong, the bridge was opened just three weeks before the stadium.

TOP: Artwork in the East Stand.

MIDDLE: Poets' corner in the East Stand.

BOTTOM: The home team changing room primed and ready for action.

ABOVE: Big screen TVs are tested.

Neil Burchell

Seeing the first arch arrive filled me with pride. It was immense! This wasn't going to be just another new ground. It was going to be special. A ground of hope and glory.

Things you didn't know about the Amex

Wide angle

The two giant screens in the stadium are the first of their kind in the UK.

ABOVE: Club staff pose for a team photo taken from the gantry.

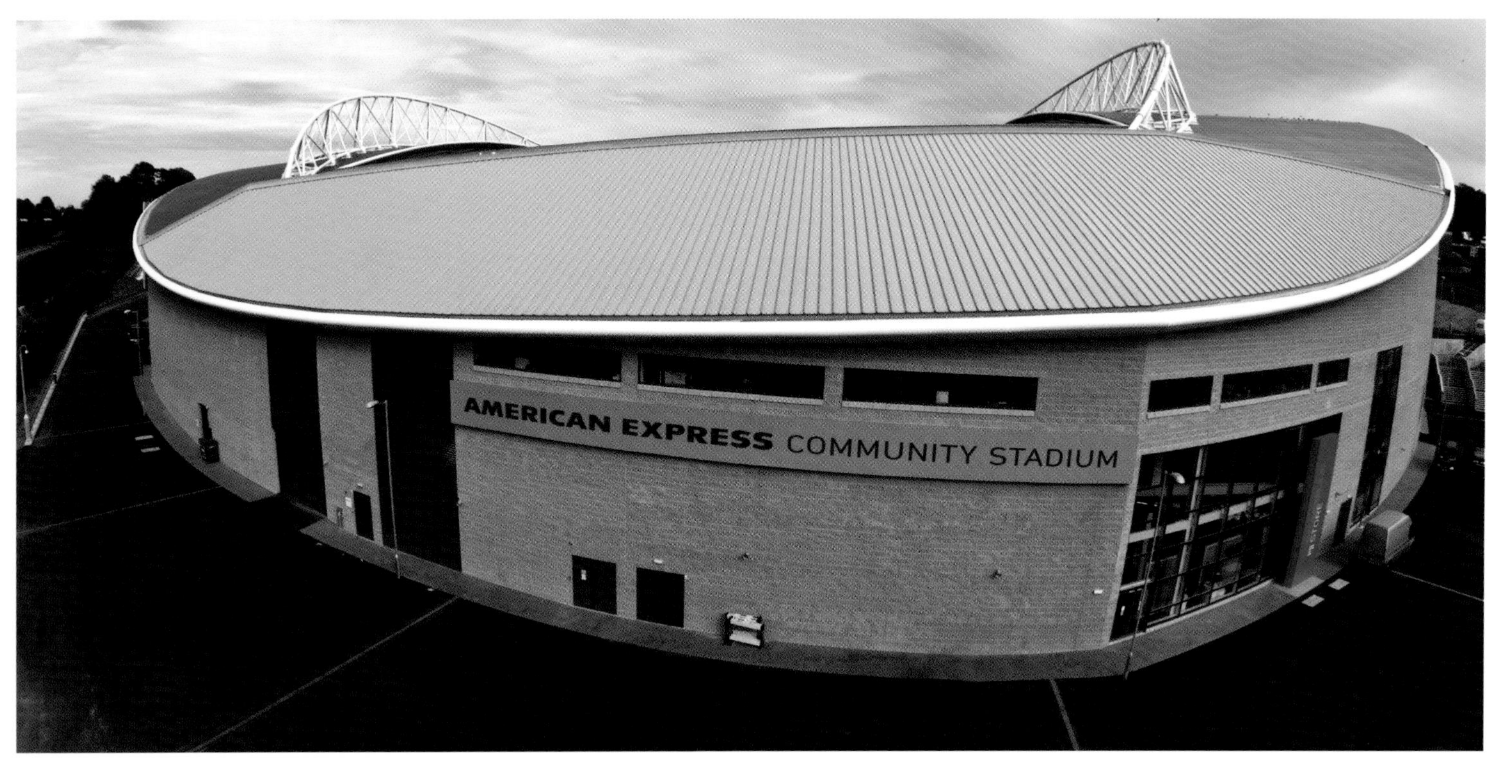

TOP: Final signage installation to the North Stand.

BOTTOM: Stadium exterior photographed from a cherry picker on the concourse.

ABOVE: Arriving in style. The West Stand reception is open.

Pass it

10,000 lanyards were ordered for entry passes.

Courtney Hazlewood

Bigger and better than the mighty Goldstone Ground. A stadium I could only dream about, absolutely breathtaking!

Martin Perry

We were delighted that major companies in Brighton & Hove came forward to sponsor the various lounges including Bupa Insurance Services, Profile (Brighton) Ltd, Rossett Beck Group and Lifestyle Europe. The Chairman named the Lower Gold South Lounge after his grandfather Harry Bloom in memory of his time as Deputy Chairman at the club. A number of other companies including American Express have also taken individual executive boxes.

Things you didn't know about the Amex

Amex Chef

The Amex Head Chef, Fred Tobin, was once personal chef to a British Prime Minister.

 ABOVE: Hospitality suites ready for guests.

ABOVE: The Bupa Lounge laid up and ready for the first time.

33
27
35
23
31
15

ABOVE: Ready for action. Players inspect the pitch prior to the inaugural friendly against Spurs.

errea
Donatello
errea
errea
errea

ABOVE: Fans proudly wearing blue and white stripes for the big day.

Things you didn't know about the Amex

Staff

1,100 staff work at the stadium on match days.

 ABOVE: Cheers. We did it!

Things you didn't know about the Amex

14,083

14,083 pints of beer (and 670 packets of crisps please) were served at the first match against Spurs.

ABOVE: Fan inspired mosaic adorning the wall of Dick's Bar.

 ABOVE: The West Stand starts to fill in anticipation.

Things you didn't know about the Amex

Bangers

1,320 sausages are consumed on a match day.

ABOVE: Fans arriving for the big day.

Things you didn't know about the Amex

4,651

Who ate all the pies? Brighton fans did... 4,651 of them at the friendly match against Spurs.

ABOVE: Home at last.

Financial Services
Business Insurance
A&A
CONSTRUCTION
GROUP
20 40 60 TAXI 205 205
skint
Brighton and
HoveJobs.com
SKINT

Darren Balkham

People have protested and marched, always with humour, getting the attention of the greater football family in the name of Brighton & Hove Albion. This stadium is credit to those who marched and to those no longer with us.

ABOVE: Fans bask in the summer sun.

ABOVE: A picture paints a thousand words.

seagulls.co.uk
MORTGAGES ON TAP
THE PROFILE LOUNGE
Porsche Centre Mid-Sussex
Leaders
First In Letting
seagulls.co.uk
BECKS PEUGEOT
Light Bros
Brewers
CROWN
LanGuard
PORTSLADE PANELWORKS
IT First
CAR PARTS
PARKER BUILDING SUPPLIES
20 40 60 TAXI 205 205
Burt Family Butchers Ltd
The Argus
Sun Harvest Ltd
The Argus
The Argus

ABOVE: The team is presented together with Club Chairman Tony Bloom and his son Josh, proud mascot for the occasion.

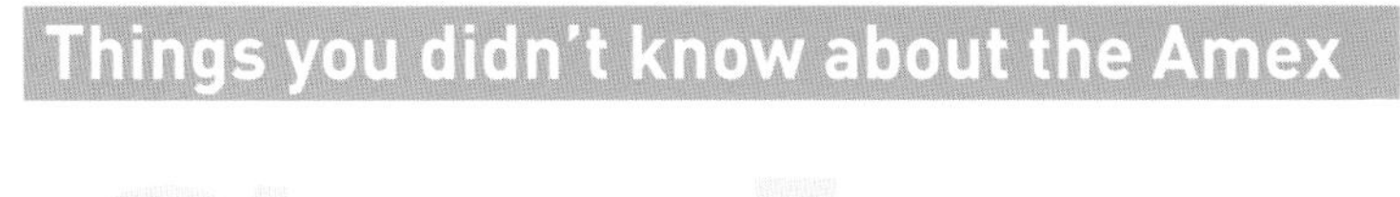

Things you didn't know about the Amex

Corker

215 bottles of wine were quaffed at the first match against Tottenham Hotspur.

ABOVE: Fans are presented with the two teams immediately prior to kick off.

A1 BECKS PEUGEOT
seagulls.co.uk
LanGuard
20 40 60 TAXI 205 205
SEAGULLS Player
EastCentral Brasserie
Matchday bistro cuisine
restaurantbrighton@azure.uk.com | 01273 878282
agulls.co.uk

 ABOVE: Men of Steel.

STADIUM